Discover you own special
Birthstone
and
the renowned Healing Powers of
Crystals

Robert W. Wood D.Hp
(Diploma in Hypnotherapy)

Rosewood Publishing

First published in U.K 1999
By Rosewood Publishing
P.O. Box 219, Huddersfield,
West Yorkshire HD2 2YT

www.rosewood-gifts.co.uk

Copyright © 1999

Revised cover and
Re-printed in 2011

Robert W Wood D.Hp
asserts the moral right to be identified
as the author of this work

Copy-editing
Margaret Wakefield BA (Hons) London
www.euroreportage.co.uk

Cover photograph by
Andrew Caveney BA (Hons)
www.andrewcaveneyphotography.co.uk

Cover and layout re-designed by
AJ Typesetting
www.ajtype.co.uk

Printed in Great Britain by
Delta Design & Print Ltd
www.deltaleeds.co.uk

ISBN 978-0-9532930-0-1

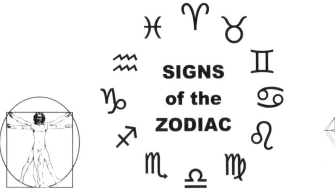

SIGNS of the ZODIAC

Awake to a glorious world of mystery.
By looking into your heart
you will find the truth, who you are,
what is right and what is not,
always remembering that beauty and
goodness exist in everything.

BIRTHSTONES

The Greeks gave us the now-familiar twelve signs of the Zodiac, but it was Carl Gustav Jung who, at the turn of the century, successfully linked his special form of psychology with astrology. He was interested to show how the collective and individual expressions of energy could be linked with the signs of the Zodiac.

It is a little known fact that, while your sun sign generally reflects your outward image, it would appear that your opposite sign reveals the true 'inner' you. Try it: first read your own star sign, and then read your opposite.

See if Jung is right!

ARIES   21st Mar - 20th Apr   Birthstone: RED JASPER

The Ram   The First House (ruled by MARS)

Element: **FIRE**

Key Phrase:

I HAVE TO KNOW WHO I AM

Arians have a straightforward and positive attitude to life. They need adventure and like to take risks. They are passionate and sexy people but can be aggressive and dominating.

Positive traits: Courageous, enthusiastic, independent, forthright, active, energetic

Negative traits: Extravagant, impulsive, brash, selfish, impatient, headstrong

TAURUS   21st Apr - 21st May   Birthstone: ROSE QUARTZ

The Bull   The Second House (ruled by VENUS)

Element: **EARTH**

Key Phrase:

I NEED TO SEE WHAT I AM

Taureans are very loyal, sensible and reliable, but need security and routine in their lives. They are passionate lovers but can be very possessive and stubborn.

Positive traits: Sincere, reliable, stable, faithful, solid, dependable

Negative traits: Obsessive, intransigent, possessive, naive, obstinate, plodding

GEMINI   22nd May - 21st Jun   Birthstone: BLACK ONYX

The Twins   The Third House (ruled by MERCURY)

Element: **AIR**

Key Phrase:

I NEED TO KNOW WHAT I AM

Very chatty, lively people who make good salespeople, with a natural ability to sell. Geminis can be charming, flirty and fun, but can be impatient with others.

Positive traits: Humorous, communicative, ingenious, witty, versatile, spontaneous

Negative traits: Emotionally detached, inclined to exaggerate, flighty, restless, fickle

CANCER   22nd Jun - 22nd Jul   Birthstone: MOTHER OF PEARL

The Crab   The Fourth House (ruled by the MOON)

Element: **WATER**

Key Phrase:

I MUST KNOW MY ORIGINS

Real Cancerians are very nice, caring and sensitive, with a tendency to worry. They can be moody but are very faithful and supportive to partners.

Positive traits: Industrious, thrifty, loyal, sympathetic, sensitive, tenacious

Negative traits: Secretive, capricious, cloying, over-emotional, touchy, clinging

LEO   23rd Jul - 23rd Aug   Birthstone: TIGER EYE

The Lion   The Fifth House (ruled by the SUN)

Element: **FIRE**

Key Phrase:

I AM CAPABLE OF BECOMING MORE

Leos are leaders and organisers who love life. They are generous and like to spend money. They can be dominating and very vain, but can also be warm and enthusiastic.

Positive traits: Benevolent, hospitable, forgiving, affectionate, regal, magnanimous

Negative traits: Self-centred, uncompromising, vain, gullible, domineering

VIRGO   24th Aug - 22nd Sep   Birthstone: CARNELIAN

The Virgin   The Sixth House (ruled by MERCURY)

Element: **EARTH**

Key Phrase:

I MUST ALWAYS STRIVE FOR PERFECTION

Virgoans are workers, practical and neat in every way. They can be perfectionists and critical of others. They are also very genuine people who tend to worry.

Positive traits: Painstaking, analytical, studious, considerate, discriminating

Negative traits: Self-effacing, prone to worry, detached, sceptical, cynical

4

LIBRA 23rd Sep - 23rd Oct Birthstone: **GREEN AVENTURINE**
The Scales The Seventh House (ruled by VENUS)
Element: AIR This is the sign of fair play and harmony. Librans are charmers who enjoy socialising and do not like to feel left out. They manage to appear calm in situations, but can be indecisive.
Key Phrase:
I MUST JUSTIFY Positive traits: Gracious, cheerful, charming, refined, diplomatic
MY EXISTENCE Negative traits: Manipulative, procrastinating, indecisive, impressionable

SCORPIO 24th Oct - 22nd Nov Birthstone: **RHODONITE**
The Scorpion The Eighth House (ruled by MARS & PLUTO)
Element: WATER Scorpios are energetic, intense, sensual people. They enjoy positions of power and are very searching. They are secretive and jealous, with a tendency to be over-possessive with partners, but enjoy an active sexual relationship.
Key Phrase: Positive traits: Resourceful, decisive, penetrating, persuasive, competitive, focused
I AM NOT ALONE Negative traits: Resentful, vindictive, sarcastic, jealous, suspicious, cunning

SAGITTARIUS 23rd Nov - 21st Dec Birthstone: **SODALITE**
The Centaur The Ninth House (ruled by JUPITER)
Element: FIRE Hunters, who need freedom and stimulation. Sagittarians are enthusiastic and fun-loving, with a thirst for knowledge. They need a lot of understanding as they can be unreliable and restless, especially within the confines of a relationship.
Key Phrase: Positive traits: Frank, logical, kind, generous, optimistic, honest
I LOVE TO LIVE Negative traits: Extravagant, quarrelsome, blunt, dictatorial, irresponsible

CAPRICORN 22nd Dec - 20th Jan Birthstone: **OBSIDIAN SNOWFLAKE**
The Goat The Tenth House (ruled by SATURN)
Element: EARTH Capricorns are ambitious, hard-working, independent individuals who enjoy good taste. They have a tendency to be bossy and stubborn, with a need for financial security and stability.
Key Phrase:
NIL Positive traits: Profound, patient, practical, efficient, ambitious, hard-working
DESPERANDUM Negative traits: Gloomy, snobbish, materialistic, arrogant, intolerant, pessimistic

AQUARIUS 21st Jan - 19th Feb Birthstone: **BLUE ONYX**
The Water Carrier The Eleventh House (ruled by SATURN & URANUS)
Element: AIR Aquarians make excellent friends as they are understanding and faithful. They are complex characters, original and magnetic. They can appear eccentric at times, and have lively traits.
Key Phrase:
I BELONG TO THE Positive traits: Humane, trustworthy, caring, intuitive, friendly, broad-minded
FAMILY OF MAN Negative traits: Unpredictable, moody, rebellious, stubborn, abrupt, impersonal

PISCES 20th Feb - 20th Mar Birthstone: **AMETHYST**
The Fish The Twelfth House (ruled by JUPITER & NEPTUNE)
Element: WATER Pisceans are creative and imaginative but sometimes lack confidence.
Key Phrase: They are very caring, sensitive, kind characters. Lack of ambition is one of
I WISH I COULD their negative traits, together with vagueness and indecision.
COME BACK Positive traits: Unassuming, courteous, artistic, imaginative, gentle, lenient
SOME OTHER TIME Negative traits: Apologetic, irrational, changeable, self-pitying, hypersensitive

Is there
Hidden Power in Gemstones?
Judge for yourself!

The idea of being cured by a lump of rock may sound crazy, but it is said that precious gems have been doing that since the dawn of time.

Does it work? The only evidence is from the people who believe it does.

However, scientific research has shown an amazing fact: that each type of crystal vibrates at a different frequency. For example, a digital watch works because of a small piece of quartz vibrating at a constant frequency, stimulated by energy from a battery.

Experts believe that our bodies can act like a battery. We can stimulate crystals in such a way that they can have a beneficial effect on our well-being.

It is said that if we place crystals close to us, our bodies will tune in to the vibrational frequency and be energised and healed.

If you have a gas oven, you may use a special lighter wand to create a spark. This tool has a piece of quartz built into it, which releases energy (the spark) when used, without any need of a battery.

One of the simplest ways to benefit from crystal power is to wear one or carry one in your bag or pocket, and at night take it to bed with you. It is believed that each stone emits a certain energy which is beneficial - but only if the wearer is receptive to its energies.

Thought patterns create energy. Positive thought is amplified by using a quartz crystal combined with our own natural healing power. This can bring much relief to many conditions.

It is said to be more a case of the stones finding us than us finding them, so if you feel attracted to a particular stone then you will benefit far more if you use that stone.

Once found, your stone should be cleansed before use. This can be done by simply cleaning it with cool water and then allowing it to dry naturally in the open air.

You can either hold it in your hand or at the side of you; relax, take a moment, and imagine your body, your mind and your crystal all in perfect harmony. This can be more beneficial if done last thing at night and first thing in the morning for a period of at least 10 days. You will then be in a position to answer the question 'Is there hidden power in gemstones?' for yourself.

THE HEALING POWER OF CRYSTALS

N.B. The following information is not authoritative, but a fluid interpretation from many sources.

1. RED JASPER
A powerful healing stone. Can help those suffering from emotional problems by balancing physical and emotional need; its power to give strength and console such sufferers is well known.
Good for: liver, kidneys, bladder. Improves the sense of smell.

2. ROSE QUARTZ
Healing qualities for the mind. Gives help with migraine and headaches. Excites the imagination. Helps release pent-up emotions; lifts spirits and dispels negative thoughts. Eases both emotional and sexual imbalances. Increases fertility.
Good for: spleen, kidneys and circulatory system. Coupled with Hematite, works wonders on aches and pains throughout the body.

3. BLACK ONYX/AGATE
Can give a sense of courage, and helps to discover truth. Instils calm and serenity. Gives self control whilst aiding detachment.
Good for: bone marrow, relief of stress.

4. MOTHER OF PEARL
Aptly dubbed the 'sea of tranquillity'. Creates physical harmony of a gentle but persuasive kind. Calms the nerves. Indicates treasure, chastity, sensitivity and strength.
Good for: calcified joints, digestive system.

5. TIGER EYE
The 'confidence stone'. Inspires brave but sensible behaviour; fights hypochondria and psychosomatic diseases.
Good for: liver, kidneys, bladder. Invigorates and energises.

6. CARNELIAN
'The friendly one' - a very highly-evolved healer. A good balancer, can connect with your inner self. Brings good concentration, joy, sociability and warmth.
Good for: rheumatism, depression, neuralgia. Helps regularise the menstrual cycle.

CARNELIAN/AMETHYST

The Carnelian, when coupled with Amethyst, purifies the consciousness, reverses negative thoughts and develops higher mental awareness. Good for: shaking off sluggishness and becoming vigorous and alert.

7. GREEN AVENTURINE

Stabilises through inspiring independence, well-being and health. Acts as a general tonic on the physical level. A stone to encourage a higher level of meditation. Favoured by Carl Fabergé, the Russian craftsman famous for Fabergé Eggs. A talisman, a bringer of good fortune. Good for: skin conditions; losing anxiety and fears.

8. RHODONITE

Improves memory; reduces stress. Gives confidence and self-esteem. Cheers the depressed, preserves youth and retards the ageing process. Helps to bring back the life force into the sick. Carries the power to the unobstructed love. A very special stone. Good for: emotional trauma, mental breakdown; spleen, kidneys, heart and blood.

9. SODALITE

Calms and clears the mind, enhancing insight and communication with the higher self. Brings joy and relieves a heavy heart. When placed at the side of the bed, it can make a sad person wake up full of the joys of spring. Imparts youth and freshness to its wearer. Good for: When combined with Rhodonite, can produce the 'Elixir of Life'.

10. OBSIDIAN SNOWFLAKE

For all those it recognises, it is a powerful healer. Keeps energy well grounded, clears subconscious blocks and brings and insight and understanding of silence, detachment, wisdom and love. A lucky talisman, a bringer of good fortune. Favoured by ancient Mexican cultures to neutralise negative magic. Good for: eyesight, stomach and intestines.

11. BLUE ONYX/AGATE

Improves the ego. A supercharger of energy; a stone of strength and courage. Aids concentration and helps to soothe all kinds of hostile feelings, allowing joy into your life. Inspires serenity. Good for: stress; certain ear disorders.

12. AMETHYST
Aids creative thinking. Relieves insomnia when placed under pillow. A very special and powerful aid to spiritual awareness and healing. Very helpful for meditation, inspiration, intuition and divine love. When worn with Carnelian it will calm the overactive. A 'love and romance' stone.
Good for: blood pressure, fits, grief, insomnia.

13. HEMATITE
A stone you either like or dislike. To those who like it, it can be a very optimistic inspirer of courage and magnetism. Lifts gloominess and depression. When used in conjunction with Carnelian it can prevent fatigue. This stone is particularly effective during pregnancy.
Good for: blood, spleen; generally strengthens the body.

14. ROCK CRYSTAL
This stone holds a place of unique importance in the world of gems. It enlarges the aura of everything near to it and acts as a catalyst to increase the healing powers of other minerals. Its vibrations resonate with a triple-time, waltz-like beat of life, giving it a co-ordinating role in all holistic practices. It is the stone most favoured for crystal gazing.
Good for: brain, soul; dispels negativity in your own energy field.

15. MOONSTONE
Gives inspiration and enhances the emotions. A good emotional balancer; a solid friend, inspiring wisdom. In India the Moonstone is a sacred gem, thought to be lucky if given by the groom to his bride.
Good for: period pain and kindred disorders, fertility and childbearing.

A GUIDE TO THE POWER WITHIN

POWER GEMS

A unique group of Gemstones and Crystals, carefully linked in harmony to unite their individual mystic powers and provide a Holistic Force which can revive Health, increase Wealth, bring Peace and provide Energy.

The concept of being treated by a lump of rock may sound odd and hard to imagine, but ancient civilisations have been doing just that since the dawn of time.

Traditions, myths and supernatural stories have always been associated with the magical mysteries of Crystals, Minerals and Gemstones. For thousands of years, people have told extraordinary stories about the power that has come from within these stones.

The Sumerians and Babylonians, then the Egyptians and the Greeks, and even our own English ancestors not only believed in these healing properties, but actually used crystals and gemstones for treating a wide range of ailments and conditions in everyday life.

These ancient beliefs may have been lost or rebuffed for the last few hundred years, but some of these legends have now been proven to be close to the truth. Remarkable stories of complete recoveries after years of pain and misery are now becoming commonplace.

If just one crystal or gemstone does possess such power and does have such a potency, then just imagine how exciting the prospect is, of having three crystals and gemstones linked together. The thought of such power from each stone, united with the powers of others and amplified, is awesome.

Most Power Gems contain three gemstones or crystals, a powerful number, being representative of Mother Earth as well as the Holy Trinity.

POWER GEM TITLES

HEALER
We have united the three most powerful healing Gemstones and Crystals.

CARNELIAN
The friendly one. It is a very highly evolved healer, mentioned many times in both the Old and New Testaments of the Bible.

RED JASPER
Well known as a powerful healing stone and a provider of strength. Mentioned in the New Testament in Revelations 21:19 – "The first foundations of the walls of the New Jerusalem were made of Jasper". Represents Aries in Astrology, the first energy of the life cycle – "On the first day of Spring, a commencement force of purest energy revitalises the Earth".

ROCK CRYSTAL
This stone holds a place of unique importance in the world of gems. It enlarges the aura of everything near to it and acts as a catalyst to increase the healing powers of other minerals. Co-ordinates all holistic practices.

Power Phrase :- Healing

GOOD LUCK
The three most powerful Gemstones, known for their good fortune.

OBSIDIAN SNOWFLAKE
Favoured by ancient Mexican cultures to neutralise negative magic. A very lucky talisman, a bringer of good fortune.

GREEN AVENTURINE
Green is a colour associated with God, and in Astrology is linked with Libra. Libra is the cardinal Air sign of the Zodiac and Air is the Breath of Life. Libra is also the seventh sign of the Zodiac, which is also favoured as God's number. Green Aventurine was favoured by Carl Fabergé, the Russian craftsman famous for "Fabergé Eggs".

MOONSTONE
In India, Moonstone is a sacred gemstone and is given to the bride by the groom on their wedding day, as a token of good luck and fortune. The moon has the most influence and power of all the heavenly bodies over our Earth.

Power Phrase :- My luck's returned, I give thanks.

ADULTS ONLY
These powerful stones combine to create the most imaginative aphrodisiac. A very sensuous combination.

ROSE QUARTZ
Well known as a love stone with a beautiful colour of pink.

AMETHYST
A romantic stone, very helpful for meditation, inspiration and divine love.

CARNELIAN
A stone used on the breastplate of King Solomon. This power stone represents passion and energy and, like Amethyst, Carnelian contains iron traces which give it its seductive colour. A solid, dependable stone.

Power Phrase :- Bring my lover to me

FOR WILLPOWER
The most powerful combination of stone and crystal which can be used to boost the willpower, e.g. to lose weight or stop smoking.

ROSE QUARTZ
Healing qualities for the mind, helps to release pent up emotions whilst dispelling negative thoughts.

BLACK ONYX
It can give a sense of courage and helps to discover truth. Gives self control, whilst aiding detachment. Helps relieve stress.

ROCK CRYSTAL
This stone holds a place of unique importance in the world of gems. It enlarges the aura of everything near to it and acts as a catalyst to increase the healing powers of other minerals. Co-ordinates all holistic practices.

Power Phrase :- I can and I will

TO REMOVE ACHES AND PAINS
Three Gemstones designed for easing aches and pains.

ROSE QUARTZ
Rose Quartz is made up of minute crystals with traces of Titanium, a metallic element, which give it profound strength.

HEMATITE
There are many ailments which benefit from a source of iron. When united with Rose Quartz, this steel-like stone works wonders with aching bones and bruised skin.

ROCK CRYSTAL
Once again the power of Rock Crystal acts as a catalyst to increase the active powers within Rose Quartz and Hematite.

Power Phrase :- Healing light, shine on me.

PEACE OF MIND

A combination of stones to bring peace, harmony and tranquillity into your surroundings, to capture stillness in movement.

GREEN AVENTURINE
Green is said to be God's colour. A stone well known for easing anxiety and fears. A talisman, a bringer of good fortune.

ROSE QUARTZ
A love stone, which also helps to relieve migraine and headaches. Releases pent up emotions and high spirits, and dispels negative thoughts.

RHODONITE
Improves memory, calms the mind, reduces stress, gives confidence and self-esteem. Cheers the depressed, preserves youth and retards the ageing process. A very special stone.

Power Phrase :- Relax

ENERGY BOOSTER

A combination of three Gemstones to boost energy.

CARNELIAN
Good for shaking off sluggishness and helping us to become more vigorous and alert. A Gemstone used on the breastplate of King Solomon, maybe to boost his energy, perhaps because, as we know, he had 1,000 wives. Carnelian is associated with Virgo, the sixth sign of the Zodiac, and the element Earth.

AMETHYST
When coupled with Carnelian, Amethyst becomes a very powerful energy booster. Amethyst is tinted by irradiated iron, and iron is one of the six active body minerals essential for life. It strengthens muscles, enriches the blood and increases resistance to illness.

ROCK CRYSTAL
Has the power to enlarge the aura of other Gemstones, and in this case it increases power to store energy. In Greek mythology, Rock Crystal was known as Holy Water, frozen by the gods of Olympus.

Power Phrase :- Energy, Vitality and Strength

www.rosewood-gifts.co.uk

TO LIFT DEPRESSION
Three Gemstones which bring joy and happiness, and remove sadness.

CARNELIAN
The friendly one. Carnelian is a highly evolved healing stone. Provides good concentration, and brings joy, sociability and warmth.

HEMATITE
To those who like it, it can be a very optimistic inspirer of courage and personal magnetism. Lifts gloominess and depression.

TIGER EYE
Inspires brave but sensible behaviour. The confidence stone, fights hypochondria and psychosomatic diseases.

Power Phrase :- From sorrow to joy

ELIXIR OF LIFE
To produce an Elixir of Life, we should first wash the Gemstones, then place them in a glass of clear water and leave them overnight, ideally in the light of a full moon. The Elixir of Life should be sipped slowly in a ritualistic manner. This is a powerful approach, which appeals directly to the imagination.

RHODONITE
Preserves youth and retards the ageing process. Helps to bring back the life force into the sick, carries the power to the unobstructed love. A very special stone.

SODALITE
Brings joy and relieves a heavy heart. Imparts youth and freshness to its wearer.

Power Phrase :- Life force, grow in me.

IMAGINE
I used the lovely title from John Lennon's song "Imagine", as these stones really are designed for a very special purpose. Power beyond imagination holds the key to all changes of life. The fine tints of these stones are designed to help us reach a level within the mind where all things become possible.

ROSE QUARTZ
Helps to excite the imagination; helps to relieve pent up emotion. Lifts spirits and dispels negative thoughts.

AMETHYST
Aids creative thinking. A very special and powerful aid to spiritual awareness. Very helpful for meditation, inspiration and intuition.

GREEN AVENTURINE
Green is said to be God's colour. Stabilises through inspiring independence. A stone to encourage a higher level of meditation.

Power Phrase :- Imagination

POWER GEMS

POWER BEYOND IMAGINATION

Many scholars and philosophers have stated that man is master of his own destiny.

Man has fully mastered his environment: planet earth, the land, the seas and the skies. He can travel around his world at will. He has built bridges and dug tunnels; he can travel both under and over water; he can fly higher and faster than any bird; he has travelled millions of miles in space, and has successfully been to the moon and back.

What makes man so special? He has learned to use the power of imagination, from deep inside the subconscious part of his mind, to conquer his environment and create the machinery to conquer the whole planet.

Having knowledge of the powers of your subconscious mind leads straight to the super-highway of the mind, which brings forth all kinds of riches, including spiritual, mental and physical, as well as financial.

Understand that energy, translated into thoughts, emotions and feelings, is the cause of all our experience, and so the cause of all effects.

With this powerful thought in mind, we should learn how to use this powerful subconscious power - a power that can heal the sick, lift fear and depression, and free us from the restrictions of poverty, want and misery. It can break the chains of repression for ever.

All we have to do is to be quite clear of the needs we wish to embody, and the creative powers of our subconscious mind will respond accordingly. Draw deep upon the 'power beyond imagination', and you will uncover a completely new experience.

The Bible says, in a simple, clear and beautiful way: 'Whosoever shall say unto this mountain: be thou removed, and be thou cast into this sea; and shall not doubt in his heart, but shall believe that those things which he saith shall come to pass; he shall have whatsoever he saith.

Therefore I tell you, whatever you ask for in prayer, believe that you have received it, and it will be yours.'
MARK 11:23

In learning how to use our inner powers, we can open the prison doors of fear and enter into a life described by Paul as 'the glorious liberty of the sons of God'.

DISCOVER THE MAGIC WITHIN THE MIND

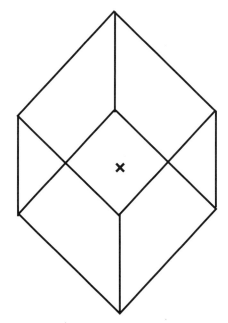

JUST LOOK AT THE CROSS FOR A WHILE AND SEE THE PICTURE CHANGE. YOU WILL THEN HAVE EXPERIENCED THE WORKING OF THE MAGIC WITHIN THE SUBCONSCIOUS MIND.

POWER GEMS
Three Magic Steps

STEP ONE
Find a peaceful and quiet place. Relax completely; empty your mind of the worries of the day. Relax into a sleepy, drowsy state, but try not to fall asleep. In this relaxed, peaceful, receptive state we are now ready for step two.

STEP TWO
Concentrate on a short phrase - a 'power phrase' - which you can easily remember and repeat over and over again, like a lullaby or Mantra. This can be done within the quiet of your mind, or, better still, spoken softly out loud. This will help it to enter your subconscious mind. Repeat this for five or more minutes, three or four times each day.

STEP THREE
As you are going to sleep each night, practise the following technique. Repeat your 'power phrase' - for example, 'Health' - quietly, easily and feelingly. Do this over and over again, just like a lullaby. Lull yourself to sleep with the word 'Health'. Within a short period, your life should start to be transformed. You will be amazed at the result. Your health should improve dramatically, thus proving you have control of the power of your subconscious mind.

To ensure the most effective enforcement of your affirmation, you should also repeat STEP THREE first thing in the morning as you awake, and touch your Power Gem lightly. Once you can instinctively touch your stones and repeat your 'power phrase' on waking, you have arrived at a level of mind that will bring about all the changes you desired.

The phrase 'Health' can be substituted by any one of the other power phrases. The appropriate Power Gem should be at your bedside at all times.

See your local stockist first, for any Gemstones and Crystals mentioned in this publication.

For further details - write to:
Rosewood
P.O. Box 219, Huddersfield, West Yorkshire. HD2 2YT
E-mail enquiries to: **info@rosewood-gifts.co.uk**
Or why not visit our website for even more information:
www. rosewood-gifts.co.uk

Other titles in the 'POWER FOR LIFE' series:

A Special Glossary of Healing Stones plus Birthstones REF. (BK2)
An introduction to Crystal Healing, with an invaluable Glossary listing common ailments and suggesting combinations of Gemstones/Crystals.

Create a Wish Kit using a Candle, a Crystal and the Imagination of Your Mind REF. (BK3) 'The key to happiness is having dreams; the key to success is making dreams come true.' This book will help you achieve.

Gemstone & Crystal Elixirs – Potions for Love, Health, Wealth, Energy and Success REF. (BK4) An ancient form of 'magic', invoking super-natural powers. You won't believe the power you can get from a drink!

Crystal Pendulum for Dowsing REF. (BK5) An ancient knowledge for unlocking your Psychic Power, to seek out information not easily available by any other means. Contains easy-to-follow instructions.

Crystal Healing – Fact or Fiction? Real or Imaginary? REF. (BK6) Find the answer in this book. Discover a hidden code used by Jesus Christ for healing, and read about the science of light and colour. It's really amazing.

How to Activate the Hidden Power in Gemstones and Crystals REF. (BK7) The key is to energise the thought using a crystal. The conscious can direct – but discover the real power. It's all in this book.

Astrology: The Secret Code REF. (BK8) In church it's called 'Myers Briggs typology'. In this book it's called 'psychological profiling'. If you read your horoscope, you need to read this to find your true birthstone.

Talismans, Charms and Amulets REF. (BK9) Making possible the powerful transformations which we would not normally feel empowered to do without a little extra help. Learn how to make a lucky talisman.

A Guide to the Mysteries surrounding Gemstones & Crystals REF. (BK10) Crystal healing, birthstones, crystal gazing, lucky talismans, elixirs, crystal dowsing, astrology, rune stones, amulets and rituals.

A Simple Guide to Gemstone & Crystal Power – a mystical A-Z of stones REF. (BK11) From Agate to Zircon, all you ever needed or wanted to know about the mystical powers of gemstones and crystals.

Change Your Life by Using the Most Powerful Crystal on Earth REF. (BK12) The most powerful crystal on earth can be yours. A book so disarmingly simple to understand, yet with a tremendous depth of knowledge.

All the above books are available from your local stockist,
or, if not, from the publisher.

NOTES

Welcome to the world of Rosewood

An extract from a 'thank- you' letter for one of my books.

"I realised just how much you really had indeed understood me and my need for direction and truly have allowed me the confidence and strength to know and believe I can achieve whatever I want in life"

If you like natural products, hand-crafted gifts including Gemstone jewellery, objects of natural beauty – the finest examples from Mother Nature, tinged with an air of Mystery – then we will not disappoint you. For those who can enjoy that feeling of connection with the esoteric nature of Gemstones and Crystals, then our 'Power for Life – Power Bracelets could be ideal for you. Each bracelet comes with its own guide explaining a way of thinking that's so powerful it will change your life and the information comes straight from the Bible. e.g. read Mark 11: 22

We regularly give inspirational talks on Crystal Power – fact or fiction? A captivating story about the world's fascination with natural gemstones and crystals and how the Placebo effect explains the healing power of gemstones and crystals – it's intriguing. And it's available on a CD

To see our full range of books, jewellery and gifts including CD's and DVD'S

Visit our web site - www.rosewood-gifts.co.uk

To see our latest videos go to 'You Tube' and type in Rosewood Gifts.